D1359429

You've Got This

You've Got This

101 ways to boost your
confidence, nurture
your spirit and remind
yourself that everything
is going to be okay

Domonique Bertolucci

Hardie Grant

BOOKS

For Sophia and Tobias

and

*For anyone who has ever doubted themself
and needed a gentle reminder that everything
really is going to be okay.*

The Mindset Mantras

*I know what I want and I'm willing
to work for it.*

I honour my values and let them guide me.

*I recognise all that I have and express
gratitude regularly.*

I believe in myself and my right to be happy.

I trust myself and recognise my potential.

*I accept responsibility for how things are
and how I would like them to be.*

I love my life.

Introduction

*What if I'm not good enough? What if
something bad happens?
What if I don't have enough? What if
I miss out?
What if I can't do enough? What if they don't
like me?
What if I get it wrong? What if they talk
about me?
What if I am not enough?*

The one thing each of these questions has in
common is that they are speculative; they are
about what *if* – not what *is*.

They are worries, not facts.

Many years ago I made the decision not to worry.

Growing up, both my mother and my childhood bestie were worriers. And to me it seemed they were indiscriminate in their worries. They worried about anything and everything: things that might go wrong, the impact of things that might go right, and everything in between.

I loved them both with all my heart, but as I looked at these two women, one young and one considerably older, I decided that while there would be much I could learn from them in life, on this particular topic – worrying – class was definitely dismissed. So having decided that worrying wasn't going to work for me, I set out to find a better way.

As I began my journey towards adulthood, I absorbed everything I could about personal growth, discovering that, contrary to what most people thought, it wasn't our feelings that ruled our world, it was our thoughts – and if we chose them consciously, we could control how we felt about the world.

I discovered the power of my *mindset* – the set of thoughts I could create that would determine how I experienced my life. Over time I developed a set of *mindset mantras* that became the belief system for my life. From that point on, if something concerned me, I would examine the situation using the mindset mantras as my guide – if I could do something about it, I did, and if I couldn't, I simply let it go.

I'd love to tell you I never experienced worry again but that wouldn't be true. I am pleased to say, though, that it has become such a rare occurrence that I can't remember the last time I did.

At the beginning of this book I've shared the *mindset mantras* that work best for me – but in the following pages I've included more than one hundred of these mantras so that any time you find yourself feeling worried or anxious, you can choose new, more powerful thoughts: thoughts that work for you, not against you.

But please don't save this book just for life's tough times. My sincerest hope is that these pages become thin and worn because choosing your thoughts becomes something you do every day.

If you would like to learn more about changing your mindset, and developing and creating thoughts and feelings that help you navigate your way through life, you can download a printable copy of The Mindset Mantras and join my mini-course on how to put them into action in your daily life. You can access both at domoniquebertolucci.com/life.

I am already
all that I will ever
need to be.

I am enough

While seeking to grow and evolve is valuable,
aiming to be perfect is simply not achievable.

If you find yourself worrying that you
are not good enough or that your efforts are
going to fall short in some way, take a deep
breath and remember that, although you may
be imperfect, you are perfectly imperfect just
the way you are.

*I value myself and
expect others to respect me.*

I am worthy

If you are feeling unsure of yourself or insecure, sometimes it may feel easier to accept less than what you know you deserve.

Next time you are negotiating or asking for what you want, don't let anyone short-change you. Remember that it is only by understanding your true worth that you have any chance of receiving it.

*I choose to
see beyond myself.*

I practise acceptance

No matter how hard you wish for it, not everything in life is going to turn out the way you want. In fact, sometimes things may go completely and utterly wrong.

Next time you find yourself deeply disappointed by life, instead of feeling like a victim and asking 'Why me?', remind yourself that the situation may actually have very little to do with you and everything to do with the fact that, sometimes, things just happen.

*I believe that success
is coming my way.*

I am committed

Working hard doesn't mean you will instantly get what you want. So often in life there is a timing difference between your effort and your reward.

If you are feeling like you want to give up, don't. Keep going and remind yourself that while right at this moment you might not have the success you want, if you quit now you never will.

*I believe in myself and
the good that I bring.*

I am a good person

Everybody makes mistakes sometimes and although it can feel awful at the time, your mistakes don't define you.

Instead of beating yourself up when you've done something wrong, forgive yourself, do what you can to make things right and then refocus your energy on all the things you do well – and for which you will never need any forgiveness.

*I know what I want
and I'm willing to work for it.*

I take action

It's easy to spend your time dreaming about what you want from life, but it is much harder to take action to make it happen.

Next time you find yourself thinking about the dreams you have for your future, take a minute to choose one small step you can take right at that moment that will take you closer to the life you dream of.

*I accept failure as a
step in my journey
towards success.*

I am resilient

While having a goal or clear intention can feel incredibly motivating, sometimes, no matter how hard you try or how focused you are, you simply aren't able to achieve it.

When this happens, remember that although you may not have reached your target, *you* are not a failure, just someone who is still working towards success.

I am braver than I feel.

I have courage

Being brave isn't always easy. Sometimes you might find yourself in a situation where you feel like you are going to need more courage than you have.

Next time you find yourself feeling this way, remember that courage isn't a finite resource and the best way to increase yours is with regular acts of bravery.

I am generous in my
opinion of others.

I see the best in others

Although most people are doing their best most of the time, not everyone will get everything right all of the time – no matter how hard they try. And when they do get it wrong, and it has an impact on you, it can be especially frustrating.

If you find you are frustrated or annoyed by someone else's mistake, instead of focusing on the things they are getting wrong, focus on who they are as a person and recognise all the things they are attempting to get right.

*I treat myself with
love, kindness and respect.*

I accept myself

Any time you find yourself judging your appearance, your abilities or any other aspect of yourself, stop. Ask yourself if you would be such a harsh critic of a friend or loved one.

Instead of speaking harshly to yourself, accept your imperfections and treat yourself with the same love, kindness and respect you give to other important people in your life.

*I value my wellbeing
and make it a priority.*

I take time to recharge

When you live a busy life, it's easy to feel pulled in so many different directions that you feel depleted before you're even halfway through the day.

If you catch yourself feeling spent before you've even begun, take some time out to do something for yourself. Instead of feeling guilty about pressing pause, see this time as an investment – one that will reward you with more energy to do everything else that needs to get done.

*I believe my life
will be a happy one.*

I deserve joy

Sometimes life sends an experience your way that feels irrecoverable and you find yourself barely able to breathe, let alone able to imagine ever being truly happy again.

If you find yourself feeling this way, it's important to remember that simply holding yourself upright and putting one foot in front of the other is all you need to expect of yourself right now.

Although you may never 'get over' this loss or change, know that in time you will get used to the pain, and it will no longer have the power to get in the way of your happiness.

*I accept my body
and am thankful for the life
it is giving me.*

I embrace my body

No matter how well you take care of yourself, your body will change over time and according to life's circumstances. Sometimes you may end up not liking your body as much as you once did.

If you find yourself feeling this way, remind yourself that whatever its shape or size, your body has served you well up until now. Rather than engaging in negative self-talk and criticising or hating your body, embrace it, acknowledging that you would like it to continue serving you for many more years to come.

*I stand up for
what I think is right.*

I use my voice

It would be nice if every conversation in life could be all sweetness and light, but the truth is, sometimes a difficult conversation is exactly what the situation calls for.

When you need to deliver a dose of tough love, instead of agonising over how the other person will react, focus your attention on what you want to say and how you are going to say it. This will give them the best chance of actually hearing it.

*I have the courage
to explore all my options
and choose the one
that is right for me.*

I have choices

There is no such thing as having 'no choice'. The thing that paralyses most people is the fear of making the *wrong* one.

If you find yourself struggling to make a decision, instead of feeling that you have no choice or worrying that you will make the wrong one, remind yourself that you always have options, then give yourself permission to fully explore them.

*I am willing to take
imperfect action today
instead of waiting forever
for a perfect tomorrow.*

I do what I can

There are times in life when everything seems to fall perfectly into place and you have all the resources you need to get things to turn out exactly the way you want them to.

Unfortunately, those times don't come along every day, so instead of waiting for everything to be perfect, decide that, as imperfect as things are, you are going to do the best you can with what you've got.

*I channel my energy
towards making my life
better for myself.*

I use my energy wisely

Although worrying doesn't change anything, it is still very easy to waste a lot of time and energy doing it.

When you catch yourself churning over something that's troubling you, stop. Take the energy you are spending on worrying and put it to much better use – work out how to resolve your concern or do something that distracts you from it entirely.

*I appreciate
all that is good
about my life.*

I like my life

When you look around you, both in real life and online, you can easily fall into the trap of thinking that everyone else has got it together, and that their lives are running much more smoothly than yours.

But they are not. The image most people share on social media is a half-truth at best. Next time you find yourself thinking like this, instead of allowing comparison-itis to eat away at your happiness, focus your attention on what you do have and what is working for you. Appreciate your life for all that it is.

*I am open-minded
and willing to respect
people's differences.*

I am respectful

While it is important to surround yourself with people who share your values, you will find you still have to spend at least some of your time interacting with people who don't.

When you come across someone you don't understand or with whom you don't see eye to eye, instead of being quick to judge them as wrong, make a conscious choice to recognise that their perspective simply isn't one that's right for you.

*I believe in myself
and trust my intentions.*

I am confident

It can be incredibly nerve-racking to place yourself at the front of the pack or to put yourself forward as an example to others.

In situations like this, remember that, no matter how hard you try, you may not be able to make everyone happy or impress them with your efforts. Instead of seeking the approval of others, focus on what you want to gain from this opportunity, and put your energy into making sure you get it.

*I prioritise my needs and
take care of myself.*

I am self-ist

There is nothing selfish about wanting to take some time for yourself, but it's easy to forget this when other people want your time and attention.

Next time you find yourself feeling guilty about taking some me-time, remember that being selfish means putting your needs first to the detriment of others, whereas being self-ist simply means that you recognise that your needs matter too.

*I accept my challenges and
rise to meet them.*

I am strong

Some days are harder than others, sometimes for good reason and other times just because.

When you feel like simply getting through the day is an uphill battle, remind yourself that it is only when you get to the peak that you will be able to see beyond your current challenges and out to the wide world that awaits you.

*I treat my body
with kindness and respect.*

I nurture my body

It isn't always easy to eat what you know you should be eating when there are so many temptations around. But while the occasional treat or indulgence is an enjoyable part of life, continually over-indulging is not a healthy way to live.

Next time you're tempted to reach for food that comforts you, or gives you a short-term high, take a minute to listen to what your body really needs and then choose something nourishing that answers that need instead.

*I admire and respect
the person I am.*

I like myself

While most people are kind and respectful, not everyone you interact with will be. When someone shuts you down or is dismissive of you, it's easy to worry that the problem is you.

Next time you find yourself worrying about what you did wrong or why they don't like you, remind yourself that while you might prefer it if they did like you, what matters far more is that *you* like you.

*I always make the
right decision for me.*

I trust my judgement

When you have a decision to make, it's easy to tie yourself in knots trying to make sure you get it right. But the truth is, for most things in life there is no one right decision, and the only wrong decision is indecision.

If you are faced with a decision, instead of trying to see into the future and worrying if you'll get it right, take a deep breath and trust yourself to make the best choice for you right now, based on all the information you have.

*I always do my best
and I know my best is
good enough.*

I do my best

When you are committed and motivated, there will always be more you could do, ways you could improve or things you could change.

Next time you find yourself worrying that you could have done more or tried harder, remind yourself perfection is an impossible goal and that as long as you do your best today, your best was good enough for today.

I accept my fears and recognise them as proof that something matters.

I care deeply

Don't read more into feelings of fear or worry than they deserve. These uncomfortable feelings are usually nothing more than signs that something is important to you.

If you find yourself feeling this way, remind yourself that there is nothing wrong with wanting something to go well – what is unhealthy is spending your time and energy fretting that it won't.

*I feel good about my life
and have gratitude for
all it has given me.*

I am thankful

Not everything in life is going to go your way. There will be times when you miss out, feel let down or are disappointed by the way things turn out.

Instead of dwelling on these times and giving them greater weight than they deserve, refocus your attention on all the good things that have already come your way and all that you really do have to feel grateful for.

*I always act with
the best intentions.*

I act with love

When you feel responsible for someone else's happiness, health or wellbeing, you can easily fall into the habit of prejudging every step you take and every decision you make.

Caring for a loved one, young or old, is not always an easy task, so rather than second-guess your every move, trust that as long as you are doing your best, your loved ones are lucky to have you.

*My opinion of myself
is the only one
that matters to me.*

I appreciate myself

It can be easy to fall into the trap of worrying about what other people are going to think or say about you, when the truth is, they're usually too busy thinking about themselves to give you much thought at all.

Next time you find yourself meeting people for the first time, and worrying what they're going to think of you, stop. Your opinion of yourself is the one that really matters, so remind yourself of all that you like about you.

*I am committed to
creating harmony in my life.*

I value balance

Living a balanced life does not mean that you have to achieve balance every minute of every day, it's something that you need to maintain over time. Even the most balanced of lives will have days or even weeks that are out of whack.

When you find yourself feeling out of balance, don't panic. Know that maintaining balance in life is like balancing at the middle of a seesaw: it only works if you continue to make constant adjustments. So take a deep breath and look for your next opportunity to shift things back to where they need to be.

*I am willing to grow
from everything I experience.*

I seek wisdom

When things go wrong in your life, well-meaning people will often say, 'Everything happens for a reason'. While this might sound good on a fridge magnet, when your world is caving in, it can be the last thing you want to hear, let alone put yourself under pressure to feel.

The fact is, bad things usually don't happen for a 'reason' – they just happen. Next time you find yourself in the midst of a crisis, take comfort in knowing that while these events may not have happened for a 'reason', in time you will have the opportunity to find your own reason or meaning in them.

I see beauty everywhere,
including when I look
in the mirror.

I see beauty

When you look in the mirror, it can be easy to zoom in on all the things that you consider less than perfect about your face or your body.

Instead of falling into the trap of seeking physical perfection and constantly falling short, remind yourself that true beauty is never just skin deep. Accept any imperfections you may see and remind yourself that no matter what they are, they can never detract from the unique beauty that is you.

*I always act with kindness
and respect for others.*

I am supportive

When you have to give criticism or negative feedback, or need to have a challenging conversation with someone, it can be easy to get caught up in what you want to say.

When you are preparing for a difficult conversation, instead of focusing on what you want to say, shift your attention to what you want them to hear and how you want them to feel. This will help you to get your message across and get them to actually receive it.

*I only need to
answer to myself.*

I own my choices

Next time you find yourself worrying that someone is going to judge you or disapprove of your efforts, remind yourself that the only person you ever really need to satisfy is yourself.

If you make decisions that are aligned with your values and support the things that matter most to you, you can be confident that whatever anyone else may think, you have chosen precisely the right option for you.

*I recognise my efforts
and acknowledge myself
for making them.*

I celebrate my success

When you've put your heart and soul into something, it can be easy to fall into the trap of waiting for someone else to tell you how good it was, and for your sense of success to depend entirely on that feedback.

Waiting for external validation is a risky game. You might get it – but then again you might not. Whenever you are feeling pleased with your efforts, instead of playing chicken with your self-esteem, take a minute to congratulate yourself and celebrate all you have achieved.

*I confidently take
the action I need
to create the life I want.*

I am brave

Sometimes creating the life you want will require you to take risks, expose yourself to failure and leave you questioning if you've got what it takes.

Next time it feels like your knees are knocking, remind yourself that being nervous or unsure is a reflection of how you are feeling and has no bearing at all on what you are capable of doing.

*My life is filled
with abundance.*

I am wealthy

How you experience wealth in your life is about so much more than how much money you have or don't have. Feeling wealthy is a state of mind, one that you can activate by recognising all the abundance in your life.

You will start to feel wealthy when you recognise that you have more than you need in many areas of your life. So if you find yourself slipping into a poverty mentality, remind yourself that regardless of how much money you have in your pocket, you probably already have more than you need in your life.

*I look at others with
an open mind and
an open heart.*

I am forgiving

Nobody enjoys being on the receiving end of someone else's callous words or careless actions, but it hurts even more when it's someone who really matters in your life.

If someone you care about has hurt your feelings, remind yourself that people are a complex mix of experiences and emotions, and good people sometimes let themselves down. Although this doesn't excuse their behaviour or make it acceptable, it may help you to see it as forgivable.

*I guard my self-esteem
like the precious resource it is.*

I protect my self-esteem

If you find yourself in a bout of negative self-talk and criticism, stop. Although you may feel you are running over the 'facts', all you are really doing is running down your self-esteem.

When you catch yourself doing this, instead of trampling on your self-esteem, exchange your negative cycle for a positive one. Remind yourself that although nothing has more power than your subconscious to tear yourself down, nobody in the world is better placed than you are to build yourself back up again.

*I am present to
each and every day of my life.*

I live in the moment

Regardless of whether it is with positive expectation or anxious anticipation, spending all your time thinking about the future will prevent you from enjoying the present.

If you find yourself focusing on tomorrow and what *might* happen, make the decision to shift your attention and energy to today, and refocus on what *is* happening.

I always do the right thing,
no matter how much courage it takes.

I have integrity

Sometimes life presents you with a sticky situation, moral quandary or ethical dilemma where you know that although there is an easy way out, it wouldn't be the right way out.

The next time your integrity is challenged, make the decision to do the right thing. Regardless of how things turn out, you will be able to look back and be proud that you had the courage to do what needed to be done.

*I accept the passing of time
with grace.*

I embrace my age

While some people seem to have bodies that can defy time, most of us find that as we age our bodies change – and not always in ways we would like.

Instead of raging against the sinking and sagging the future is likely to bring, appreciate your body the way it is today and remind yourself that in ten years' time you will probably wish it was the way it is right now.

*I easily disengage
from conflict when I see that
it is not serving me.*

I am willing to let go

Regardless of how it started, when you find yourself caught up in an argument it can quickly become a verbal tug of war. The best way to end a tug of war is just to let go – and so it is with arguments, regardless of who is at fault.

If you find yourself caught up in an argument, instead of holding on in the hope of victory, let go and, at the very least, be willing to meet the other person halfway.

*I always know
what is right for me.*

I have the answer

When you are feeling conflicted about a choice, it can often seem easier to look outside yourself for the answer. But whether it's canvassing friends for their opinion or searching for the right answer online, all you're really doing is abdicating responsibility for the decision you need to make.

When next you have an important decision to make, instead of taking this outward approach, shift your attention inwards. Trust that you already know the right answer, you just need the courage to sit quietly and listen for it.

*I focus my
attention wherever
it is needed most.*

I do what matters

It's only when you commit to doing what really needs to be done that you realise how unimportant the rest of your list actually is.

Next time you find yourself caught up in a whirlwind of busyness and feel overwhelmed by all you have to do, stop. Instead of trying to juggle a million and one things, and feeling like you've failed at each, choose something that really matters and give it one hundred per cent of your attention until it is done.

*I trust myself and
recognise my potential.*

I face my fears

When you decide you want more out of life, one of the first things you will have to do is leave your comfort zone behind.

If you need to say farewell to your comfort zone, remind yourself that it's okay to feel nervous, anxious or afraid of leaving but that having those feelings is never a reason to stay.

I make the most of the opportunities that surround me.

I am fortunate

There is nothing lucky about having a good life. While everyone is presented with different opportunities, the opportunities themselves rarely matter as much as what you choose to do with them.

Next time you find yourself wishing you were luckier, or wanting your stars to align, remind yourself that luck is something you make, and then go out and do what you can to create it.

*I choose relationships
that support and nurture me.*

I protect myself

You can't choose your family. But you can choose the relationship you have with them. As a child you are at the mercy of your family dynamic, but as an adult you get to decide how you want things to play out.

If you find you need to put some space between you and your family, remind yourself that as an adult you are perfectly entitled to do it.

*I have faith in myself
and in my abilities.*

I back myself

No matter how much you might wish it, not everyone will be supportive of you all of the time. Rather than wait for other people to rally round, it's up to you to be your biggest fan.

Next time you feel that nobody is on your side, whatever you do, don't give in and join their team. Instead, be your own biggest cheerleader and don't stop until you cross the finish line.

*I nurture my body,
mind and soul, and know that
I am dependent on all three
for my happiness.*

I take care of myself

Taking time to attend to your mental and emotional healing is important if you want to maintain a happy and healthy outlook on life.

Nurturing your mental and emotional health is just as important as taking care of your physical health. Just as you would bandage a wound if it needed it, don't be afraid to wrap yourself in metaphorical cotton wool next time you need to.

*I know how to keep going
when I need to.*

I am determined

If things aren't going your way, it can be easy to think that the answer is to walk away; after all, regardless of the challenge, giving up will always be the easier option.

Next time you feel like quitting, ask yourself if you're doing this because it is the easy option or because it is the right one. If it's the right one, then do it. But if you know leaving would mean quitting before you're really done, take a deep breath, dust yourself off and get back into the ring again.

*I embrace new opportunities
to grow and change.*

I am willing to grow

Stepping out of your comfort zone can be nerve-racking; it is called a 'comfort' zone for a reason. But it is only when we try new things or step up to new challenges that we discover what we are truly capable of.

When you are faced with an opportunity to try something new, accept it willingly, and know that, fail or succeed, the one thing you can be certain of is that you will never find it quite so uncomfortable again.

*I am always willing to
see the other side of the story.*

I have perspective

There are always two sides to every story, but when you are in the middle of it all, it can be easy to forget that yours isn't the only point of view.

If you find yourself engaged in conflict of any kind, take a minute to shift your perspective to the other person's point of view. While this might not instantly resolve the conflict, it might be just what you need to help you navigate your way through it.

*I always know
the right next step
for me.*

I trust myself

Unless someone is living your life, their criticisms, well intended or otherwise, will always be based on their own values, expectations and experiences.

If you find yourself trying to work out what to do, instead of attempting to do what other people think is right, trust in your ability to know your own right answer and commit to doing what you believe is best for you.

*I am committed to
taking action.*

I do what it takes

Sometimes that last thing you feel like doing is the one thing you know you need to do. But regardless of whether it is a physical, mental or emotional challenge, don't make the mistake of waiting until you feel motivated to take action.

When you find yourself struggling to get going, remind yourself that it's your results that fuel your motivation and not the other way around. Then, instead of waiting, give yourself the nudge you need to go out and do what needs to be done.

*I am willing to love
and be loved.*

I am open to love

When you've been deeply hurt in the past, it can be hard to put yourself out there again and trust enough to give someone else a chance.

If you find yourself closing off or shutting down to protect yourself, remind yourself that while emotional injuries can be deeply painful, they aren't fatal. Although there is the risk of history repeating itself, if you don't open yourself up, you will never have the chance to have your future recreate itself.

*I recognise the wealth
and abundance in my life.*

I am blessed

When you are bombarded with images from the media – social or otherwise – it is easy to focus on the things that are missing in your life.

If you catch yourself feeling this way, instead of thinking about something you might lack or something you wish you had, focus on all you do have and all you have to be grateful for.

*I accept the choices
of others.*

I am caring

Everyone is on their own journey in this life and the only path you can ever be responsible for is your own.

If a friend or loved one is on a journey that concerns you, remember that while it may be your duty of care to warn them, it is not your responsibility to divert them.

*I have no need
to see myself as better or
worse than anyone else.*

I am equal

There is no point comparing yourself with anyone else. Regardless of the measure, there will always be someone with more – and there will always be someone with less.

If you realise you are looking outside yourself to measure your worth, stop. Take responsibility for your self-esteem and choose to fuel it from within.

*I treat myself with
love and care.*

I nurture myself

There's nothing wrong with feeling like you need some kind words and a hug when things aren't going your way, but, unfortunately, you can't always get that support just when you need it.

Next time you're having a bad day or going through a tough time, remind yourself that sometimes all you need is to be wrapped up in a big hug, and sometimes you're the only one who can do it.

*I meet my challenges
with determination and grit.*

I persevere

Sometimes the things you want most
are really hard to achieve and require all
the dedication and determination you
can muster.

Next time you find yourself facing a
challenge, instead of dreaming about a time
when it might be easier to tackle and waiting
for that magical day to come, accept that it
will be hard and go on and do it anyway.

*I look forward to
the future as it unfolds.*

I accept change

Being forced to make changes or having new situations thrust upon you can be confronting.

When you are forced to take a different path than the one you had intended, instead of resenting or resisting this change, remind yourself that life is always evolving. Instead of trying to change things that are beyond your control, seek out the opportunities this new situation holds.

*I am focused on the things
I can change and let go of
the things I can't.*

I am at peace

There is very little that we can genuinely control in this life – especially if other people are involved. If we feel like we are in control, usually this is an illusion. At best, all we have is influence.

Next time you feel like you are banging your head against a wall trying to force a situation you really have no power over, stop. Work out which part of the situation you can genuinely influence and then let go of the rest.

I am free to
change my mind
whenever it feels right to me.

I choose my path

When you've worked hard towards something and it is finally in your sights, sometimes you may find that you don't really want it after all.

If this happens to you, instead of thinking it has all been a wasted effort or that you need to stick with it because of that effort, remind yourself that your goals, hopes and dreams are your own and you can do anything you want with them – including walking away.

*I'm willing to fall over
because I know I can
get back up again.*

I am persistent

Everyone fails sometimes – and sometimes, no matter how hard you try, you fail over and over again.

If you find this happening, the most important question to ask is 'Do I still want this?' If your answer is 'Yes!', keep doing the work, be willing to fail and know deep down that with every failure you are one step closer to success.

*I am honest with myself
about who I am and
how I feel.*

I accept my feelings

When you bottle up your feelings, all you are really doing is increasing the chance that they will bubble up and spill over – or worse, explode.

Feelings like anger, jealousy or rage lose a lot of their intensity when you accept them, so next time you find these feelings are bubbling to the surface, don't try to swallow or stifle them. Instead, allow yourself to fully acknowledge them and watch them settle back down again.

*I am happy for others
and take pleasure in their enjoyment.*

I have a generous spirit

When you see someone doing something you want to do, or having something you wish you had, it can be easy to let the green-eyed monster get the better of you.

If you find yourself feeling envious of someone else's achievements, experiences or possessions, choose generosity over jealousy and express your admiration instead.

*I seek out people who
understand and encourage me.*

I am supported

When you decide to be the best you can be and take responsibility for your own happiness, the circle of people who understand your path often contracts.

If this happens to you, rather than looking around and lamenting those who are not walking beside you, spend as much time as you can with people who have already made the decision to walk alongside you.

*I only accept thoughts
that support me.*

I choose my thoughts

Listen to the voice inside your head. If it
is speaking to you with any less support or
encouragement than your best friend would
give you, it's time for a shift in your mindset,
to reprogram yourself to be your own best
counsel, biggest cheerleader and best friend.

Next time the voice in your head berates
you or puts you down, silence it and tell it to
get with the program instead.

*I am committed to
honouring my needs.*

I respect myself

When you are generous with your time, it is easy to find yourself saying yes to every request for help and support. So much so that, if you are not careful, you'll have given so much of yourself away that you have nothing left for you.

Sometimes the hardest commitment to honour is the one you have made to yourself. So should you find you've said yes to too many things, remind yourself that you may need to break one of those commitments in order to keep your most important one – the one to yourself.

*I rise to the challenges
life throws my way.*

I am a survivor

Sometimes life can feel like an uphill battle, and whether it is just a bad day or a truly bad year, the challenges you are experiencing can feel like they are going to go on forever.

If you find yourself going through a tough time, remind yourself that you are capable of far more than you realise and that as hard as things might be right now, you most definitely will survive.

*I am willing
to try new things.*

I am open to new experiences

There is a fine line between feeling comfortable and being complacent. When you are genuinely comfortable, you feel content, satisfied and fulfilled. But if you are stuck in your comfort zone, you'll feel anything but.

If you feel like you are stuck in a rut, make the decision to do one thing that will take you out of your comfort zone. It doesn't matter if it is a baby step or a giant leap – all that matters is that you shake things up.

I am willing to speak up
and know I deserve
to be heard.

I stand up for myself

If you feel you're not getting enough support, respect or understanding from someone who matters to you, it's up to you to let them know their efforts are substandard.

Instead of impatiently waiting for them to work it out on their own, which will only add to your resentment and frustration, take a deep breath and tell them exactly where they are going wrong and what they need to do to get it right.

*I listen to my intuition and
trust it to guide me.*

I trust my instincts

Sometimes when you are faced with myriad options, it can almost blind you to the path ahead.

Next time you feel unclear about which way to turn, instead of looking frantically from left to right and hoping that the answer will appear, look within and allow your innate wisdom to guide you.

*I trust myself to create
the future I desire.*

I have faith

Sometimes it can feel like your future is in someone else's hands, but while the decision you are waiting on might make the path shorter, or the journey easier, only you can determine your future.

If you find yourself waiting on a decision from someone else, remind yourself that if this opportunity isn't the one for you, the right one will be just around the corner.

*I respect my feelings
but don't let them control me.*

I am kind

Next time you find yourself losing your temper or about to lose control, remind yourself that your feelings don't control your actions, your thoughts do.

Instead of lashing out, hurting someone and then feeling terrible about it, stop, breathe and think. Remember that while your feelings are yours and you are one hundred per cent entitled to them, what really matters is how much power you give them.

*I learn from my mistakes
and I forgive myself
for making them.*

I forgive myself

Even though we all know that everyone makes mistakes, it can be hard not to beat yourself up when you know you're the one who is in the wrong.

If you realise that you've messed up, let someone down or caused offence, learn from your mistake and apologise for making it. Then, instead of engaging in endless self-criticism, forgive yourself and accept it's time to move on.

*I am giving of
my time and my energy.*

I am generous

When your life is full, it can feel like there are not enough hours in the day for yourself, let alone for anyone else. But even though it may take time and energy you're not sure you have, nothing feels better than doing something for someone else.

Instead of focusing on what you need to have a good day, look around and see what you can do to make someone else's day.

*I see a future that is
full of possibility.*

I am optimistic

Sometimes your negative thoughts can seem to have a power all of their own. One minute you are indulging in one or two pessimistic possibilities and the next thing you know, your thoughts are leading you down a negativity rabbit hole.

Next time you find yourself caught in a downward spiral of negative thinking, remind yourself that if you expect things to turn out well, they usually do. It is in your best interests to be optimistic and climb back out.

*I live with meaning
and purpose.*

I am present

When you are feeling unsure of yourself and the direction your life should be taking, it is easy to get caught up looking for your 'purpose' and to give in to the temptation to put your life on hold until you find it.

If you find yourself feeling a little lost, instead of waiting until you have total clarity about what you should be doing with your life, look for meaning and purpose in the life you are living right now.

I am willing to do what it takes
to live a good life.

I create healthy habits

Few things in life feel harder at the time than breaking a habit, whether it is a physical, mental or emotional one, and going the distance can be tough.

If you need to break old habits and embed new ones, remind yourself that as hard as it feels right at that moment, if you keep it up it will soon feel like the most natural thing in the world.

*I am open to change
and look for the
opportunities it holds.*

I am willing to begin

Whether or not it was initially your choice, sometimes the only way to move forward in life is to start afresh.

If you find yourself in this situation, instead of raging against the changes you know you need to make, accept them and use the energy you have saved to make the very best of your new beginning.

*I accept my mistakes
and I am willing to
learn from them.*

I am human

Mistakes are an unavoidable part of being human; everyone makes them at different times.

Next time you discover that you have messed up, instead of berating yourself or putting yourself down, say sorry and do what you can to make things right. Remind yourself that while you are likely to continue making mistakes, if you look for the lesson learned you are unlikely to make this one again.

*I make conscious choices
that lead me towards
a happy and fulfilling life.*

I choose to be happy

Happiness is a choice, but it's not a decision you can make just once. Being happy is something you need to choose and re-choose each and every day of your life.

When you find yourself feeling frustrated or unfulfilled, examine the choices you have been making. Once you uncover the ones that aren't working, you'll know exactly what you need to change to get your life back on a happier track.

I am willing to take small steps
to get to a bigger result.

I focus on moving forward

When you've fallen way behind or let things
get out of hand, the task of getting things
back on track can feel overwhelming.

If this happens to you, rather than
focusing on the end result or looking for
the light at the end of the tunnel, shift your
attention to the smaller steps you need to
take – the ones that will light your path
along the way.

I make conscious choices
about how I think and what I feel.

I choose my experience

While you may not be able to control all the things that happen in your day, you can choose how you want to feel about them. It's up to you to decide whether to let yourself be derailed or disillusioned, or if you are going to take things in your stride and barely skip a beat.

Every morning when you wake up, think about how you want to feel and the kind of day you want to have. While you may not be able to change the events of your day, that first choice will determine how you experience them.

*I recognise all
that is good about
my life.*

I appreciate all that I have

If you find yourself looking at your life and making a long list of things you need to change, stop. Take a minute to balance this list with another list: one that recognises everything that is already good about your life.

Next time you are making plans to do things differently in your life, remember change is so much easier to create from a positive perspective; so while you're thinking about things you want to change, don't forget to think about all the things that you'd like to remain exactly the same.

*I ask for support
when I need it.*

I am loved

When people put you down or treat you dismissively, it can be hard not to take it personally. But the truth is, although not everyone you meet will like you or get you, your true kindred will love you unconditionally.

So when someone tells you that you are not all you should be, call up a loved one and ask them to remind you that you are more than you will ever need to be.

*I believe in myself
and my right to be happy.*

I am confident

Although you might not be able to control the future, you can definitely control your expectations of it. And if you focus all your attention on worrying that things might go wrong, you run the risk of never noticing when things go right.

If you find yourself worrying about what tomorrow may bring, remind yourself that you deserve an abundance of happiness and then fully expect your future to deliver it.

I deserve to be treated well and
I stand up for myself
if I need to.

I value myself

While most people in your life will probably treat you well, not everyone will get it right the first time. Whether intended or otherwise, if someone gives you less respect than you deserve, it is up to you to stand up for yourself.

Next time you find yourself preparing to excuse someone for their behaviour, take a deep breath and call them out on it. Remind yourself that while it might be uncomfortable and you might need to be brave, your self-esteem depends on it.

*I focus my attention
on things I can change.*

I am proactive

When you are unhappy about a situation, the easiest option is to get angry but then do nothing. Anger alone rarely leads to an improvement and, more often than not, ends up making things worse.

When something isn't going your way, rather than wasting your energy raging against it, work out what you can do about it and switch your energy and attention to that instead.

I am doing all that I can
with all that I have.

I am dedicated

Although waiting for a situation to be perfect before you take action might feel like an easier path, it will never lead you anywhere.

Next time you find yourself waiting for the timing to be right or to have all your ducks in a row, remember that imperfect action will always take you further than taking no action at all.

*I like the person I am
and so do the people
who matter to me.*

I am accepted

There is nothing worse than the feeling you get when you've let yourself or someone else down.

If something happens that makes you feel like a fool, don't berate yourself or call yourself horrible names. Imagine the support and advice your best friend would give, and comfort yourself instead.

*I honour my values and
let them guide me.*

I know what matters

Throughout your life you will be presented with a wide range of options and opportunities. Rather than let these choices overwhelm you, use your values, the things that matter most to you, as your beacon or guiding light.

When you're having to weigh up your options, instead of compiling a list of pros or cons, ask yourself, 'Will this option take me closer to, or further from, my happiest and most fulfilling life?' and then let your values guide your way.

*My efforts determine
my experience.*

I am willing to try

There's no denying it, sometimes the stakes are really high and the thing you are working towards matters more than usual.

When you're faced with a situation like this, remind yourself that while you can't control the outcome, you can control your effort. Take a deep breath, give it all you've got and be proud of yourself for trying.

*I recognise my mistakes as
a chance to grow.*

I am willing to learn

There's nothing quite like that feeling you get in the pit of your stomach when you discover that you've made a mistake.

Next time that happens to you, remind yourself that the reason you feel so bad about getting it wrong is because you are the kind of person who does what they can to get things right. Instead of silently fretting about it, focus your attention on the learning opportunity your mistake has given you.

*I recognise all that I have
and express gratitude regularly.*

I am grateful

When you want something that is out of your reach financially, it's easy to fall into the trap of feeling that you are poor, when in reality you already have everything you fundamentally need, and no doubt have a significant amount of what you want.

If you find yourself feeling glum about the things you can't afford or that you want more of, remind yourself of all the things you already have in abundance.

*I accept responsibility
for how things are and
how I would like them to be.*

I am fair

When you find yourself in a disagreement or conflict, it's easy to focus all your attention on the reasons why the other person is at fault. But it is only when you stop the blame game that you can start to take responsibility for the part you are playing.

When you are engaged in a conflict where you are sure the other person is to blame, ask yourself, 'How did I contribute to this mess?' And once you know your answer, you will know what you need to do to clean it up.

I see the world through
a rose-coloured lens.

I am positive

Having a positive attitude doesn't mean that you have to blindly see the world as a perfect place. Instead, apply a positive filter to your perspective so you can choose the way you want to see things.

Next time you find yourself thinking negatively about a situation or event, ask yourself whether these thoughts are helping you. If you are not confident that they are moving you forward, it is time to replace them with something that will.

*I am creating a happy
and fulfilling life for myself.*

I love my life

If you want to live a happy and fulfilling life, you need to commit fully both to creating it and maintaining it.

Next time you find yourself wanting to take an easier or more passive path, remind yourself that this is your only life and it deserves to be given all you've got.

Note from the author

I WAS ONLY a few days away from my initial deadline for this book when the world was struck by the unprecedented crisis of the coronavirus pandemic, or COVID-19 as it came to be known.

I can clearly remember feeling like the world was tipping on its axis as, almost overnight, the global situation careered out of control. Phrases that had never been part of my vocabulary, like *social distancing*, *self-isolation*, *lockdown* and *flattening the curve*, became a part of my daily conversation – and the phrase the 'new normal', which I had always used with my coaching clients to describe a new, more ideal way of being, took on a different and often heart-wrenching meaning.

At the beginning of this crisis, like a lot of people, I felt like I was holding my breath. And in those early days, more than once I found myself walking away from my computer wondering if a book like *You've Got This* would even have a place in this new emerging world.

And then I exhaled and took a fresh, deep breath.

Exhaled again.

And took another deep breath.

The situation I found myself in had challenged so many of my beliefs, none more so than the fundamental one that 'everything is going to be okay'.

But as I sat down and read my draft, not in the page-a-day way that it is designed to be read, but from start to finish, I realised that the words it contained were deeply powerful. The ability to remind yourself that, no matter what is going on in your life, 'you've got this' applies just as much in a crisis as it does in everyday life.

None of us ever knows what the future holds, but I truly believe that being able to boost your confidence, nurture your spirit and remind yourself that everything is going to be okay is more important now than ever.

I hope you find this book as helpful as I did.

Domonique

x

20 April 2020

Acknowledgements

M Y FIRST THANKS, as always, go to my wonderful agent, Tara Wynne at Curtis Brown, for her never-ending belief in my work. Thanks to Pam Brewster for your endless patience with this project, and Joanna Wong, Marg Bowman, Emily O'Neill, Patrick Cannon and all the team at Hardie Grant for giving my words such a wonderful home.

To my readers who connect with me in my Facebook group and on Instagram, thank you for sharing your experiences or simply stopping by to say hello. Hearing from you never fails to make my day.

I love my work and it is in no small part because of the people I get to share it with. To all my clients, past and present, the inspiring people who attend my workshops, those who sign up for my online programs, and my coach training students, thank you for allowing me to be a part of your life. The privilege is all mine.

To family and dearest friends, you've seen your names here before and I hope you know how important you are in my life.

A never-ending thank you to Mum, Dad and Jeff for their unconditional love and support.

To my darling Sophia and precious Toby, thank you for bringing so much love and laughter into my life.

And to Paul, for everything, always.

About the author

Domonique Bertolucci is the bestselling author of *The Happiness Code: Ten keys to being the best you can be* and six other books about happiness: what it is, how to get it and, most importantly, how to keep it.

Domonique has spent the last twenty-five years working with large companies, dynamic small businesses and everyday people, teaching them how to get more happiness, more success and more time just to catch their breath.

Prior to starting her own business in 2003, Domonique worked in the cut-throat world of high finance, where she gained a reputation as a strategic problem solver and dynamic leader. In her final corporate role, she was the most senior woman in a billion-dollar company.

Domonique's readership spans the English-speaking world, and her workshops, online courses and coach training programs are attended by people from all walks of life from all around the globe – people who want more out of life at home, at work and everywhere in between.

As well as being an accomplished professional speaker, Domonique has given hundreds of interviews across all forms of media including television, radio, print and digital media; more than 10 million people have seen, read or heard her advice.

When she is not working, Domonique's favourite ways of spending her time are with her husband and two children, reading a good book and keeping up the great Italian tradition of feeding the people that you love.

Domonique jokes that she has nearly as many passports as James Bond. She is Australian by birth, Italian by blood and British by choice. She is currently based in Sydney, Australia.

Other books by Domonique

The Happiness Code: Ten keys to being the best you can be

Love Your Life: 100 ways to start living the life you deserve

100 Days Happier: Daily inspiration for life-long happiness

Less is More: 101 ways to simplify your life

The Kindness Pact: 8 promises to make you feel good about who you are and the life you live

The Daily Promise: 100 ways to feel happy about your life

Guided journals by Domonique

Live more each day: A journal to discover what really matters

Be happy each day: A journal for life-long happiness

Free mindset training:

Download your printable copy of the Mindset Mantras and take a free short course on how to put them into action in your life:
domoniquebertolucci.com/life

Keep in touch with Domonique at:
domoniquebertolucci.com
facebook.com/domoniquebertolucci
instagram.com/domoniquebertolucci

Join Domonique's private Facebook Group for regular discussion, insights and inspiration to help you get more out of life:
Facebook.com/groups/domoniquebertolucci

For more information:
Find out more about Domonique's life coaching courses and programs:
domoniquebertolucci.com/programs

Find out more about Domonique's coach training program and become a certified professional coach:
domoniquebertolucci.com/coach-training

Published in 2021 by Hardie Grant Books,
an imprint of Hardie Grant Publishing

Hardie Grant Books (Melbourne)
Building 1, 658 Church Street
Richmond, Victoria 3121

Hardie Grant Books (London)
5th & 6th Floors
52–54 Southwark Street
London SE1 1UN

hardiegrantbooks.com

All rights reserved. No part of this publication may be reproduced,
stored in a retrieval system or transmitted in any form by any means,
electronic, mechanical, photocopying, recording or otherwise, without
the prior written permission of the publishers and copyright holders.

The moral rights of the author have been asserted.
Copyright text © Domonique Bertolucci 2021

A catalogue record for this
book is available from the
National Library of Australia

You've Got This
ISBN 978 1 74379 680 1

10 9 8 7 6 5 4 3 2

Cover design by Emily O'Neill
Typeset in Plantin Light 11/17pt by Cannon Typesetting
Printed in China by Leo Paper Products LTD.

The paper this book is printed on
is from FSC® -certified forests and
other sources. FSC® promotes
environmentally responsible, socially
beneficial and economically viable
management of the world's forests.

Hardie Grant acknowledges the Traditional Owners of the country
on which we work, the Wurundjeri people of the Kulin nation and the
Gadigal people of the Eora nation, and recognises their continuing
connection to the land, waters and culture. We pay our respects to
their Elders past, present and emerging.